Of Empire

Francis Bacon
1561–1626

Francis Bacon

Of Empire

PENGUIN BOOKS — GREAT IDEAS

PENGUIN BOOKS

Published by the Penguin Group
Penguin Books Ltd, 80 Strand, London WC2R ORL, England
Penguin Group (USA) Inc., 375 Hudson Street, New York, New York 10014, USA
Penguin Group (Canada), 10 Alcorn Avenue, Toronto, Ontario, Canada M4V 3B2
(a division of Pearson Penguin Canada Inc.)
Penguin Ireland, 25 St Stephen's Green, Dublin 2, Ireland
(a division of Penguin Books Ltd)
Penguin Group (Australia), 250 Camberwell Road,
Camberwell, Victoria 3124, Australia (a division of Pearson Australia Group Pty Ltd)
Penguin Books India Pvt Ltd, 11 Community Centre,
Panchsheel Park, New Delhi – 110 017, India
Penguin Group (NZ), cnr Airborne and Rosedale Roads, Albany,
Auckland 1310, New Zealand (a division of Pearson New Zealand Ltd)
Penguin Books (South Africa) (Pty) Ltd, 24 Sturdee Avenue,
Rosebank 2196, South Africa

Penguin Books Ltd, Registered Offices: 80 Strand, London WC2R ORL, England

www.penguin.com

The Essays first published in Penguin Classics 1985
This extract published in Penguin Books 2005

1

Taken from the Penguin Classics edition *The Essays*, edited
and introduced by John Pitcher

Set by Rowland Phototypesetting Ltd, Bury St Edmunds, Suffolk
Printed in England by Clays Ltd, St Ives plc

Contents

Contents

Of Revenge

Revenge is a kind of wild justice, which the more man's nature runs to, the more ought law to weed it out. For as for the first wrong, it doth but offend the law; but the revenge of that wrong putteth the law out of office. Certainly, in taking revenge a man is but even with his enemy, but in passing it over he is superior, for it is a prince's part to pardon. And Solomon, I am sure, saith, *It is the glory of a man to pass by an offence*.* That which is past is gone and irrevocable, and wise men have enough to do with things present and to come: therefore they do but trifle with themselves that labour in past matters. There is no man doth a wrong for the wrong's sake, but thereby to purchase himself profit or pleasure or honour or the like. Therefore why should I be angry with a man for loving himself better than me? And if any man should do wrong merely out of ill nature, why, yet it is but like the thorn or briar, which prick and scratch, because they can do no other. The most tolerable sort of revenge is for those wrongs which there is no law to remedy: but then let a man take heed the revenge be such as there is no law to punish; else a man's enemy is still beforehand, and it is two for one. Some, when they take revenge, are desirous the party should know whence it cometh. This

* From Proverbs 19.11.

is the more generous, for the delight seemeth to be not so much in doing the hurt as in making the party repent. But base and crafty cowards are like the arrow that flieth in the dark. Cosmus, Duke of Florence,* had a desperate saying against perfidious or neglecting friends, as if those wrongs were unpardonable: *You shall read* (saith he) *that we are commanded to forgive our enemies; but you never read that we are commanded to forgive our friends.* But yet the spirit of Job was in a better tune: *Shall we* (saith he) *take good at God's hands, and not be content to take evil also?*† And so of friends in a proportion. This is certain, that a man that studieth revenge keeps his own wounds green, which otherwise would heal and do well. Public revenges are for the most part fortunate: as that for the death of Caesar, for the death of Pertinax, for the death of Henry the Third of France, and many more. But in private revenges it is not so. Nay rather, vindicative persons live the life of witches, who, as they are mischievous, so end they infortunate.

---

* Cosimo de' Medici, d. 1574: the saying has not been traced.
† Job 2.10.

Of Parents and Children

The joys of parents are secret, and so are their griefs and fears: they cannot utter the one, nor they will not utter the other. Children sweeten labours, but they make misfortunes more bitter: they increase the cares of life, but they mitigate the remembrance of death. The perpetuity by generation is common to beasts, but memory, merit, and noble works are proper to men. And surely a man shall see the noblest works and foundations have proceeded from childless men, which have sought to express the images of their minds, where those of their bodies have failed. So the care of posterity is most in them that have no posterity. They that are the first raisers of their houses are most indulgent towards their children, beholding them as the continuance not only of their kind but of their work; and so both children and creatures.

The difference in affection of parents towards their several children is many times unequal, and sometimes unworthy, especially in the mother. As Solomon saith, *A wise son rejoiceth the father, but an ungracious son shames the mother.** A man shall see, where there is a house full of children, one or two of the eldest respected, and the youngest made wantons, but in the midst some that are as it were forgotten, who many times nevertheless prove

* Proverbs 10.1.

3

the best. The illiberality of parents in allowance towards their children is an harmful error, makes them base, acquaints them with shifts, makes them sort with mean company, and makes them surfeit more when they come to plenty. And therefore the proof is best when men keep their authority towards their children, but not their purse. Men have a foolish manner (both parents and schoolmasters and servants) in creating and breeding an emulation between brothers during childhood, which many times sorteth to discord when they are men, and disturbeth families. The Italians make little difference between children and nephews or near kinsfolks; but so they be of the lump, they care not though they pass not through their own body. And, to say truth, in nature it is much a like matter, insomuch that we see a nephew sometimes resembleth an uncle or a kinsman more than his own parent, as the blood happens. Let parents choose betimes the vocations and courses they mean their children should take, for then they are most flexible. And let them not too much apply themselves to the disposition of their children, as thinking they will take best to that which they have most mind to. It is true that if the affection or aptness of the children be extraordinary, then it is good not to cross it: but generally the precept is good, *Optimum elige, suave et facile illud faciet consuetudo* [Choose what is best, and habit will make it pleasant and easy].* Younger brothers are commonly fortunate, but seldom or never where the elder are disinherited.

---

* A saying ascribed to the followers of Pythagoras, in Plutarch, *On Exile*, 8 (*Moralia*, 602B).

Of Marriage and Single Life

He that hath wife and children hath given hostages to
fortune, for they are impediments to great enterprises,
either of virtue or mischief. Certainly the best works,
and of greatest merit for the public, have proceeded from
the unmarried or childless men, which both in affection
and means have married and endowed the public. Yet it
were great reason that those that have children should
have greatest care of future times, unto which they know
they must transmit their dearest pledges. Some there are
who, though they lead a single life, yet their thoughts
do end with themselves, and account future times imper-
tinences. Nay, there are some other that account wife
and children but as bills of charges. Nay more, there are
some foolish rich covetous men that take a pride in
having no children, because they may be thought so
much the richer. For perhaps they have heard some talk,
Such an one is a great rich man, and another except to it,
Yea, but he hath a great charge of children, as if it were an
abatement to his riches. But the most ordinary cause of
a single life is liberty, especially in certain self-pleasing
and humorous minds, which are so sensible of every
restraint as they will go near to think their girdles and
garters to be bonds and shackles. Unmarried men are
best friends, best masters, best servants; but not always
best subjects, for they are light to run away; and almost

all fugitives are of that condition. A single life doth well with churchmen, for charity will hardly water the ground where it must first fill a pool. It is indifferent for judges and magistrates, for if they be facile and corrupt, you shall have a servant five times worse than a wife. For soldiers, I find the generals commonly in their hortatives put men in mind of their wives and children; and I think the despising of marriage amongst the Turks maketh the vulgar soldier more base. Certainly wife and children are a kind of discipline of humanity; and single men, though they be many times more charitable, because their means are less exhaust, yet, on the other side, they are more cruel and hard-hearted (good to make severe inquisitors), because their tenderness is not so oft called upon. Grave natures, led by custom, and therefore constant, are commonly loving husbands, as was said of Ulysses, *Vetulam suam praetulit immortalitat* [He preferred his old wife to immortality].* Chaste women are often proud and forward, as presuming upon the merit of their chastity. It is one of the best bonds both of chastity and obedience in the wife if she think her husband wise, which she will never do if she find him jealous. Wives are young men's mistresses, companions for middle age, and old men's nurses. So as a man may have a quarrel to marry when he will. But yet he was reputed one of the wise men that made answer to the question, when a man should marry: *A young man not yet, an elder man not at all*. It is often seen that bad husbands have very good wives; whether it be that it raiseth the price of their husband's kindness when

---

* From Cicero, *On the Orator*, I.44.

it comes, or that the wives take a pride in their patience. But this never fails if the bad husbands were of their own choosing, against their friends' consent; for then they will be sure to make good their own folly.

Of Envy

There be none of the affections which have been noted to fascinate or bewitch, but love and envy. They both have vehement wishes; they frame themselves readily into imaginations and suggestions; and they come easily into the eye, especially upon the presence of the objects: which are the points that conduce to fascination, if any such thing there be. We see likewise the Scripture calleth envy an *evil eye*, and the astrologers call the evil influences of the stars *evil aspects*, so that still there seemeth to be acknowledged, in the act of envy, an ejaculation or irradiation of the eye. Nay, some have been so curious as to note that the times when the stroke or percussion of an envious eye doth most hurt are when the party envied is beheld in glory or triumph, for that sets an edge upon envy: and besides, at such times the spirits of the person envied do come forth most into the outward parts, and so meet the blow.

But leaving these curiosities (though not unworthy to be thought on in fit place), we will handle what persons are apt to envy others; what persons are most subject to be envied themselves; and what is the difference between public and private envy.

A man that hath no virtue in himself ever envieth virtue in others. For men's minds will either feed upon their own good or upon others' evil; and who wanteth

the one will prey upon the other; and whoso is out of
hope to attain to another's virtue will seek to come at
even hand by depressing another's fortune.

A man that is busy and inquisitive is commonly envious. For to know much of other men's matters cannot
be because all that ado may concern his own estate:
therefore it must needs be that he taketh a kind of
play-pleasure in looking upon the fortunes of others.
Neither can he that mindeth but his own business find
much matter for envy. For envy is a gadding passion,
and walketh the streets, and doth not keep home: *Non
est curiosus, quin idem sit malevolus* [No one is inquisitive
without being malevolent as well].*

Men of noble birth are noted to be envious towards
new men when they rise. For the distance is altered, and
it is like a deceit of the eye, that when others come on
they think themselves go back.

Deformed persons and eunuchs and old men and
bastards are envious. For he that cannot possibly mend
his own case will do what he can to impair another's
[. . .]

The same is the case of men that rise after calamities
and misfortunes. For they are as men fallen out with the
times, and think other men's harms a redemption of
their own sufferings.

They that desire to excel in too many matters, out of
levity and vainglory, are ever envious. For they cannot
want work, it being impossible but many in some one
of those things should surpass them. Which was the

* Plautus, *Stichus*, I.3.54.

character of Hadrian the Emperor, that mortally envied poets and painters and artificers in works wherein he had a vein to excel.

Lastly, near kinsfolks and fellows in office and those that have been bred together are more apt to envy their equals when they are raised. For it doth upbraid unto them their own fortunes, and pointeth at them, and cometh oftener into their remembrance, and incurreth likewise more into the note of others; and envy ever redoubleth from speech and fame. Cain's envy was the more vile and malignant towards his brother Abel, because when his sacrifice was better accepted there was nobody to look on. Thus much for those that are apt to envy.

Concerning those that are more or less subject to envy. First, persons of eminent virtue, when they are advanced, are less envied. For their fortune seemeth but due unto them, and no man envieth the payment of a debt, but rewards and liberality rather. Again, envy is ever joined with the comparing of a man's self, and where there is no comparison, no envy; and therefore kings are not envied but by kings. Nevertheless it is to be noted that unworthy persons are most envied at their first coming in, and afterwards overcome it better; whereas, contrariwise, persons of worth and merit are most envied when their fortune continueth long. For by that time, though their virtue be the same, yet it hath not the same lustre, for fresh men grow up that darken it.

Persons of noble blood are less envied in their rising, for it seemeth but right done to their birth. Besides, there seemeth not much added to their fortune; and envy is as the sunbeams, that beat hotter upon a bank or steep rising ground than upon a flat. And for the same reason those that are advanced by degrees are less envied than those that are advanced suddenly and *per saltum* [at a bound].

Those that have joined with their honour great travails, cares, or perils are less subject to envy. For men think that they earn their honours hardly, and pity them sometimes; and pity ever healeth envy. Wherefore you shall observe that the more deep and sober sort of politic persons, in their greatness, are ever bemoaning themselves what a life they lead, chanting a *quanta patimur* [how many things we suffer!]. Not that they feel it so, but only to abate the edge of envy. But this is to be understood of business that is laid upon men, and not such as they call unto themselves. For nothing increaseth envy more than an unnecessary and ambitious engrossing of business. And nothing doth extinguish envy more than for a great person to preserve all other inferior officers in their full rights and pre-eminences of their places. For by that means there be so many screens between him and envy.

Above all, those are most subject to envy, which carry the greatness of their fortunes in an insolent and proud manner, being never well but while they are showing how great they are, either by outward pomp, or by triumphing over all opposition or competition. Whereas wise men will rather do sacrifice to envy, in suffering themselves sometimes of purpose to be crossed and overborne in things that do not much concern them. Notwithstanding, so much is true, that the carriage of greatness in a plain and open manner (so it be without arrogancy and vainglory) doth draw less envy than if it be in a more crafty and cunning fashion. For in that course a man doth but disavow fortune, and seemeth to be conscious of his own want in worth, and doth but teach others to envy him.

Lastly, to conclude this part: as we said in the beginning that the act of envy had somewhat in it of witchcraft, so there is no other cure of envy but the cure of witchcraft; and that is, to remove the *lot* (as they call it) and to lay it upon another. For which purpose, the wiser sort of great persons bring in ever upon the stage somebody upon whom to derive the envy that would come upon themselves; sometimes upon ministers and servants, sometimes upon colleagues and associates, and the like; and for that turn there are never wanting some persons of violent and undertaking natures, who, so they may have power and business, will take it at any cost.

Now, to speak of public envy. There is yet some good in public envy, whereas in private there is none. For public envy is as an ostracism, that eclipseth men when they grow too great. And therefore it is a bridle also to great ones to keep them within bounds.

This envy, being in the Latin word *invidia*, goeth in the modern languages by the name of *discontentment*, of which we shall speak in handling sedition. It is a disease in a state like to infection. For as infection spreadeth upon that which is sound, and tainteth it, so when envy is gotten once into a state, it traduceth even the best actions thereof, and turneth them into an ill odour. And therefore there is little won by intermingling of plausible actions. For that doth argue but a weakness and fear of envy, which hurteth so much the more; as it is likewise usual in infections, which, if you fear them, you call them upon you.

This public envy seemeth to beat chiefly upon principal officers or ministers, rather than upon kings and estates themselves. But this is a sure rule, that if the envy upon the minister be great, when the cause of it in him is small, or if the envy be general in a manner upon all the ministers of an estate, then the envy (though hidden) is truly upon the state itself. And so much of public envy or discontentment, and the difference thereof from private envy, which was handled in the first place.

We will add this in general, touching the affection of envy, that of all other affections it is the most importune and continual. For of other affections there is occasion given but now and then. And therefore it was well said, *Invidia festos dies non agit* [Envy keeps no holidays], for it is ever working upon some or other. And it is also noted that love and envy do make a man pine, which other affections do not, because they are not so continual. It is also the vilest affection, and the most depraved, for which cause it is the proper attribute of the devil, who is called *the envious man, that soweth tares amongst the wheat by night;** as it always cometh to pass that envy worketh subtly and in the dark, and to the prejudice of good things, such as is the wheat.

* Matthew 13.25.

Of Love

The stage is more beholding to love than the life of man. For as to the stage, love is ever matter of comedies and now and then of tragedies; but in life it doth much mischief, sometimes like a siren, sometimes like a fury. You may observe that amongst all the great and worthy persons (whereof the memory remaineth, either ancient or recent) there is not one that hath been transported to the mad degree of love; which shows that great spirits and great business do keep out this weak passion. You must except, nevertheless, Marcus Antonius, the half-partner of the empire of Rome, and Appius Claudius, the decemvir and lawgiver: whereof the former was indeed a voluptuous man and inordinate, but the latter was an austere and wise man. And therefore it seems (though rarely) that love can find entrance not only into an open heart, but also into a heart well fortified, if watch be not well kept. It is a poor saying of Epicurus, *Satis magnum alter alteri theatrum sumus* [Each of us is enough of an audience for the other]:* as if man, made for the contemplation of heaven and all noble objects, should do nothing but kneel before a little idol, and make himself subject, though not of the mouth (as beasts are), yet of the eye, which was given him for higher purposes. It is

* Seneca, *Epistles*, VII.11.

a strange thing to note the excess of this passion and how it braves the nature and value of things, by this: that the speaking in a perpetual hyperbole is comely in nothing but in love. Neither is it merely in the phrase; for whereas it hath been well said that the arch-flatterer, with whom all the petty flatterers have intelligence, is a man's self, certainly the lover is more. For there was never proud man thought so absurdly well of himself as the lover doth of the person loved: and therefore it was well said, *That it is impossible to love and to be wise.* * Neither doth this weakness appear to others only, and not to the party loved, but to the loved most of all, except the love be reciproque. For it is a true rule that love is ever rewarded either with the reciproque or with an inward and secret contempt. By how much the more men ought to beware of this passion, which loseth not only other things, but itself [. . .] For whosoever esteemeth too much of amorous affection quitteth both riches and wisdom. This passion hath his floods in the very times of weakness, which are great prosperity and great adversity (though this latter hath been less observed); both which times kindle love and make it more fervent, and therefore show it to be the child of folly. They do best who, if they cannot but admit love, yet make it keep quarter, and sever it wholly from their serious affairs and actions of life; for if it check once with business, it troubleth men's fortunes, and maketh men that they can no ways be true to their own ends. I know not how, but martial men are given to love: I think it is but as they

* Publilius Syrus, *Sententiae*, 15.

are given to wine; for perils commonly ask to be paid in pleasures. There is in man's nature a secret inclination and motion towards love of others, which, if it be not spent upon some one or a few, doth naturally spread itself towards many, and maketh men become humane and charitable; as it is seen sometime in friars. Nuptial love maketh mankind; friendly love perfecteth it; but wanton love corrupteth and embaseth it.

Of Great Place

Men in great places are thrice servants: servants of the sovereign or state, servants of fame, and servants of business. So as they have no freedom, neither in their persons nor in their actions nor in their times. It is a strange desire to seek power and to lose liberty; or to seek power over others and to lose power over a man's self. The rising unto place is laborious, and by pains men come to greater pains; and it is sometimes base, and by indignities men come to dignities. The standing is slippery, and the regress is either a downfall or at least an eclipse, which is a melancholy thing. *Cum non sis qui fueris, non esse cur velis vivere.* [When you are no longer what you were there is no reason for wishing to live].*
Nay, retire men cannot when they would; neither will they when it were reason, but are impatient of privateness even in age and sickness, which require the shadow: like old townsmen that will be still sitting at their street door though thereby they offer age to scorn. Certainly great persons had need to borrow other men's opinions to think themselves happy, for if they judge by their own feeling they cannot find it: but if they think with themselves what other men think of them, and that other men would fain be as they are, then they are happy

* Cicero, *Letters to Friends*, VII.3.4.

as it were by report, when perhaps they find the contrary within. For they are the first that find their own griefs, though they be the last that find their own faults. Certainly men in great fortunes are strangers to themselves, and while they are in the puzzle of business they have no time to tend their health, either of body or mind. *Illi mors gravis incubat, qui notus nimis omnibus, ignotus moritur sibi* [Death lies heavily on the man who, too well known to others, dies a stranger to himself].* In place there is a licence to do good and evil, whereof the latter is a curse; for in evil the best condition is not to will, the second not to can. But power to do good is the true and lawful end of aspiring. For good thoughts, though God accept them, yet towards men are little better than good dreams except they be put in act, and that cannot be without power and place as the vantage and commanding ground. Merit and good works is the end of man's motion, and conscience of the same is the accomplishment of man's rest. For if a man can be partaker of God's theatre, he shall likewise be partaker of God's rest. *Et conversus Deus, ut aspiceret opera quae fecerunt manus suae, vidit quod omnia essent bona nimis* [And God turned to look upon the works which his hands had made, and he saw that they were all very good]:† and then the sabbath. In the discharge of thy place set before thee the best examples, for imitation is a globe of precepts. And after a time set before thee thine own example, and examine thyself strictly whether thou didst not best at first. Neglect not also the examples of those that have carried themselves

* Seneca, *Thyestes*, 401–3.   † Genesis 1.31.

ill in the same place; not to set off thyself by taxing their memory, but to direct thyself what to avoid. Reform therefore without bravery or scandal of former times and persons, but yet set it down to thyself as well to create good precedents as to follow them. Reduce things to the first institution, and observe wherein and how they have degenerate, but yet ask counsel of both times: of the ancient time, what is best; and of the latter time, what is fittest. Seek to make thy course regular, that men may know beforehand what they may expect; but be not too positive and peremptory; and express thyself well when thou digressest from thy rule. Preserve the right of thy place, but stir not questions of jurisdiction, and rather assume thy right in silence and *de facto* than voice it with claims and challenges. Preserve likewise the rights of inferior places, and think it more honour to direct in chief than to be busy in all. Embrace and invite helps and advices touching the execution of thy place, and do not drive away such as bring thee information, as meddlers, but accept of them in good part. The vices of authority are chiefly four: delays, corruption, roughness and facility. For delays: give easy access; keep times appointed; go through with that which is in hand; and interlace not business but of necessity. For corruption: do not only bind thine own hands or thy servants' hands from taking, but bind the hands of suitors also from offering. For integrity used, doth the one; but integrity professed, and with a manifest detestation of bribery, doth the other. And avoid not only the fault but the suspicion. Whosoever is found variable, and changeth manifestly without manifest cause, giveth suspicion of corruption. Therefore always when thou changest thine opinion or course, profess it plainly and declare it together with the reasons that move thee to change; and do not think to steal it. A servant or a favourite, if he be inward, and no other apparent cause of esteem, is commonly thought but a by-way to close corruption. For roughness, it is a needless cause of discontent: severity breedeth fear, but roughness breedeth hate. Even reproofs from authority ought to be grave, and not taunting. As for facility, it is worse than bribery. For bribes come but now and then; but if importunity or idle respects lead a man, he shall never be without. As Solomon saith: *To respect persons is not good, for such a man will transgress for a piece of bread.** It is most true that was anciently spoken, *A place showeth the man.*† And it showeth some to the better, and some to the worse. *Omnium consensu capax imperii, nisi imperasset* [Everyone would have thought him fit for Empire – had he never been Emperor], saith Tacitus of Galba;‡ but of Vespasian he saith, *Solus imperantium Vespasianus mutatus in melius* [Vespasian was the only Emperor who was changed for the better by empire];§ though the one was meant of sufficiency, the other of manners and affection. It is an assured sign of a worthy and generous spirit, whom honour amends. For honour is, or should be, the place

* Proverbs 28.21.
† A saying attributed to, among others, Solon and Pittacus (two of the Seven Sages of Greece).
‡ *Histories*, I.49.
§ *Histories*, I.50.

of virtue; and as in nature things move violently to their place, and calmly in their place, so virtue in ambition is violent, in authority settled and calm. All rising to great place is by a winding stair; and if there be factions, it is good to side a man's self whilst he is in the rising, and to balance himself when he is placed. Use the memory of thy predecessor fairly and tenderly; for if thou dost not, it is a debt will sure be paid when thou art gone. If thou have colleagues, respect them, and rather call them when they look not for it, than exclude them when they have reason to look to be called. Be not too sensible or too remembering of thy place in conversation and private answers to suitors; but let it rather be said, *When he sits in place, he is another man.*

Of Goodness and Goodness of Nature

I take goodness in this sense, the affecting of the weal of men, which is that the Grecians call *philanthropia*; and the word *humanity* (as it is used) is a little too light to express it. Goodness I call the habit, and goodness of nature the inclination. This of all virtues and dignities of the mind is the greatest, being the character of the Deity; and without it man is a busy, mischievous, wretched thing, no better than a kind of vermin. Goodness answers to the theological virtue charity, and admits no excess, but error. The desire of power in excess caused the angels to fall; the desire of knowledge in excess caused man to fall: but in clarity there is no excess, neither can angel or man come in danger by it. The inclination to goodness is imprinted deeply in the nature of man, insomuch that if it issue not towards men, it will take unto other living creatures: as it is seen in the Turks, a cruel people, who nevertheless are kind to beasts and give alms to dogs and birds; insomuch, as Busbechius* reporteth, a Christian boy in Constantinople had like to have been stoned for gagging in a waggishness a long-billed fowl. Errors indeed in this virtue of goodness or charity may be committed. The Italians have an ungracious proverb, *Tanto buon che val niente: So good,*

* Flemish scholar and ambassador to the Turks, d. 1592.

that he is good for nothing. And one of the doctors of Italy, Nicholas Machiavel, had the confidence to put in writing, almost in plain terms, that *the Christian faith had given up good men in prey to those that are tyrannical and unjust*.* Which he spake, because indeed there was never law or sect or opinion did so much magnify goodness as the Christian religion doth. Therefore, to avoid the scandal and the danger both, it is good to take knowledge of the errors of an habit so excellent. Seek the good of other men, but be not in bondage to their faces or fancies, for that is but facility or softness, which taketh an honest mind prisoner ... The example of God teacheth the lesson truly: *He sendeth his rain and maketh his sun to shine upon the just and unjust*;† but he doth not rain wealth nor shine honour and virtues upon men equally. Common benefits are to be communicate with all, but peculiar benefits with choice. And beware how in making the portraiture thou breakest the pattern: for divinity maketh the love of ourselves the pattern, the love of our neighbours but the portraiture. *Sell all thou hast, and give it to the poor, and follow me*;‡ but sell not all thou hast, except thou come and follow me; that is, except thou have a vocation wherein thou mayest do as much good with little means as with great, for otherwise in feeding the streams thou driest the fountain. Neither is there only a habit of goodness, directed by right reason; but there is in some men, even in nature, a disposition towards it, as on the other side there is a natural malignity. For there

* *Discourses*, II.2, Machiavelli.   † Matthew 5.45.
‡ Mark 10.21.

be that in their nature do not affect the good of others. The lighter sort of malignity turneth but to a crossness or frowardness or aptness to oppose or difficilness or the like; but the deeper sort, to envy and mere mischief. Such men in other men's calamities are, as it were, in season, and are ever on the loading part: not so good as the dogs that licked Lazarus' sores, but like flies that are still buzzing upon anything that is raw; *misanthropi*, that make it their practice to bring men to the bough, and yet have never a tree for the purpose in their gardens, as Timon had.* Such dispositions are the very errors of human nature, and yet they are the fittest timber to make great politics of; like to knee-timber, that is good for ships that are ordained to be tossed, but not for building houses that shall stand firm. The parts and signs of goodness are many. If a man be gracious and courteous to strangers, it shows he is a citizen of the world, and that his heart is no island cut off from other lands, but a continent that joins to them. If he be compassionate towards the afflictions of others, it shows that his heart is like the noble tree that is wounded itself when it gives the balm. If he easily pardons and remits offences, it shows that his mind is planted above injuries, so that he cannot be shot. If he be thankful for small benefits, it shows that he weighs men's minds, and not their trash. But above all, if he have St Paul's perfection, that he would wish to be an *anathema* from

* Timon of Athens, known as the Misanthrope, announced that since he was going to cut down a tree in his garden on which many had hanged themselves, would-be suicides should use it at once.

Christ for the salvation of his brethren,* it shows much of a divine nature, and a kind of conformity with Christ himself.

* Romans 9.3.

Of Travel

Travel in the younger sort is a part of education; in the elder, a part of experience. He that travelleth into a country before he hath some entrance into the language, goeth to school and not to travel. That young men travel under some tutor or grave servant, I allow well; so that he be such a one that hath the language and hath been in the country before, whereby he may be able to tell them what things are worthy to be seen in the country where they go, what acquaintances they are to seek, what exercises or discipline the place yieldeth. For else young men shall go hooded, and look abroad little. It is a strange thing that in sea voyages, where there is nothing to be seen but sky and sea, men should make diaries; but in land-travel, wherein so much is to be observed, for the most part they omit it; as if chance were fitter to be registered than observation. Let diaries therefore be brought in use. The things to be seen and observed are: the courts of princes, specially when they give audience to ambassadors; the courts of justice, while they sit and hear causes, and so of consistories ecclesiastic; the churches and monasteries, with the monuments which are therein extant; the walls and fortifications of cities and towns, and so the havens and harbours; antiquities and ruins; libraries; colleges, disputations, and lectures, where any are; shipping and navies; houses and gardens of state and pleasure near great cities; armories; arsenals; magazines; exchanges; burses; warehouses; exercises of horsemanship, fencing, training of soldiers, and the like; comedies, such whereunto the better sort of persons do resort; treasuries of jewels and robes; cabinets and rarities; and, to conclude, whatsoever is memorable in the places where they go. After all which the tutors or servants ought to make diligent inquiry. As for triumphs, masques, feasts, weddings, funerals, capital executions, and such shows, men need not to be put in mind of them; yet are they not to be neglected. If you will have a young man to put his travel into a little room, and in short time to gather much, this you must do. First, as was said, he must have some entrance into the language before he goeth. Then he must have such a servant or tutor as knoweth the country, as was likewise said. Let him carry with him also some card or book describing the country where he travelleth, which will be a good key to his inquiry. Let him keep also a diary. Let him not stay long in one city or town; more or less as the place deserveth, but not long: nay, when he stayeth in one city or town, let him change his lodging from one end and part of the town to another, which is a great adamant of acquaintance. Let him sequester himself from the company of his countrymen, and diet in such places where there is good company of the nation where he travelleth. Let him upon his removes from one place to another procure recommendation to some person of quality residing in the place whither he removeth, that he may use his favour in those things he desireth to see or know. Thus he may abridge his travel with much profit. As for the acquaintance which is to be sought in travel, that which is most of all profitable is acquaintance with the secretaries and employed men of ambassadors, for so in travelling in one country he shall suck the experience of many. Let him also see and visit eminent persons in all kinds which are of great name abroad, that he may be able to tell how the life agreeth with the fame. For quarrels, they are with care and discretion to be avoided. They are commonly for mistresses, healths, place, and words. And let a man beware how he keepeth company with choleric and quarrelsome persons, for they will engage him into their own quarrels. When a traveller returneth home, let him not leave the countries where he hath travelled altogether behind him, but maintain a correspondence by letters with those of his acquaintance which are of most worth. And let his travel appear rather in his discourse than in his apparel or gesture; and in his discourse, let him be rather advised in his answers than forwards to tell stories; and let it appear that he doth not change his country manners for those of foreign parts, but only prick in* some flowers of that he hath learned abroad into the customs of his own country.

* Plant.

Of Empire

It is a miserable state of mind to have few things to desire and many things to fear. And yet that commonly is the case of kings, who, being at the highest, want matter of desire, which makes their minds more languishing; and have many representations of perils and shadows, which makes their minds the less clear. And this is one reason also of that effect which the Scripture speaketh of, *that the king's heart is inscrutable.** For multitude of jealousies, and lack of some predominant desire that should marshal and put in order all the rest, maketh any man's heart hard to find or sound. Hence it comes likewise that princes many times make themselves desires, and set their hearts upon toys: sometimes upon a building; sometimes upon erecting of an order; sometimes upon the advancing of a person; sometimes upon obtaining excellency in some art or feat of the hand – as Nero for playing on the harp, Domitian for certainty of the hand with the arrow, Commodus for playing at fence, Caracalla for driving chariots,† and the like. This seemeth incredible unto those that know not the principle, *that the mind of man is more cheered and refreshed by profiting in small things*

* Proverbs 25.3.
† Nero, d. AD 68, Domitian, d. 96, Commodus, d. 192, and Caracalla, d. 217, were Roman emperors; all notorious for their great cruelties.

than by standing at a stay in great. We see also that kings
that have been fortunate conquerors in their first years,
it being not possible for them to go forward infinitely,
but that they must have some check or arrest in their
fortunes, turn in their latter years to be superstitious and
melancholy; as did Alexander the Great, Diocletian* and
in our memory Charles the Fifth† and others. For he
that is used to go forward, and findeth a stop, falleth out
of his own favour and is not the thing he was.

To speak now of the true temper of empire: it is a
thing rare and hard to keep, for both temper and distem-
per consist of contraries. But it is one thing to mingle
contraries, another to interchange them. The answer of
Apollonius to Vespasian is full of excellent instruction.
Vespasian asked him, *What was Nero's overthrow?* He
answered: *Nero could touch and tune the harp well; but in
government, sometimes he used to wind the pins too high,
sometimes to let them down too low.*‡ And certain it is that
nothing destroyeth authority so much as the unequal
and untimely interchange of power pressed too far, and
relaxed too much.

This is true, that the wisdom of all these latter times
in princes' affairs is rather fine deliveries and shiftings of
dangers and mischiefs when they are near, than solid
and grounded courses to keep them aloof. But this is but

* Roman emperor, d. 313, said to be the first sovereign to resign his
power voluntarily (he abdicated in 305).
† German (and Holy Roman) emperor, d. 1558; he abdicated the
empire in 1556.
‡ Philostratus, *Life of Apollonius*, V.28.

to try masteries with fortune. And let men beware how they neglect and suffer matter of trouble to be prepared: for no man can forbid the spark nor tell whence it may come. The difficulties in princes' business are many and great, but the greatest difficulty is often in their own mind. For it is common with princes (saith Tacitus) to will contradictories: *Sunt plerumque regum voluntates vehementes, et inter se contrariae* [The desires of kings are mostly vehement, and incompatible with one another].* For it is the solecism of power to think to command the end, and yet not to endure the mean.

Kings have to deal with their neighbours, their wives, their children, their prelates or clergy, their nobles, their second-nobles or gentlemen, their merchants, their commons, and their men of war; and from all these arise dangers, if care and circumspection be not used.

First for their neighbours: there can no general rule be given (the occasions are so variable), save one which ever holdeth. Which is that princes do keep due sentinel that none of their neighbours do overgrow so (by increase of territory, by embracing of trade, by approaches, or the like) as they become more able to annoy them than they were. And this is generally the work of standing councils to foresee and to hinder it. During that triumvirate of kings, King Henry the Eighth of England, Francis the First, King of France, and Charles the Fifth, Emperor, there was such a watch kept, that none of the three could win a palm of ground but the other two would straightways balance it, either by confederation

---

* Not Tacitus, but from Sallust, *Jugurthine War*, CXIII.1.

or, if need were, by a war, and would not in any wise take up peace at interest. And the like was done by that league (which Guicciardini saith was the security of Italy) made between Ferdinando, King of Naples, Lorenzius Medices, and Ludovicus Sforza, potentates, the one of Florence, the other of Milan.* Neither is the opinion of some of the Schoolmen to be received, *that a war cannot justly be made but upon a precedent injury or provocation.* For there is no question but a just fear of an imminent danger, though there be no blow given, is a lawful cause of a war.

For their wives: there are cruel examples of them. Livia is infamed for the poisoning of her husband; Roxolana, Solyman's wife, was the destruction of that renowned prince, Sultan Mustapha, and otherwise troubled his house and succession;† Edward the Second of England his queen‡ had the principal hand in the deposing and murther of her husband. This kind of danger is then to be feared chiefly when the wives have plots for the raising of their own children, or else that they be advoutresses.

For their children: the tragedies likewise of dangers from them have been many. And generally the entering of fathers into suspicion of their children hath been

---

* See Guicciardini, *History of Italy*, I.

† Solyman the Magnificent (or Selymus the First), Sultan of Turkey 1520–66, put his eldest son Mustapha to death at the instigation of his wife, the prince's stepmother, Roxalana. One of her own sons, Bayezid (or Bajazet), rebelled and was executed by Solyman. The Sultan was succeeded by another of her sons, Selymus II, who appeared to have none of Solyman's features or character.

‡ Isabella of Anjou, d. 1358.

ever unfortunate. The destruction of Mustapha (that we named before) was so fatal to Solyman's line, as the succession of the Turks from Solyman until this day is suspected to be untrue and of strange blood; for that Selymus the Second was thought to be supposititious. The destruction of Crispus, a young prince of rare towardness, by Constantinus the Great, his father, was in like manner fatal to his house: for both Constantinus and Constance, his sons, died violent deaths; and Constantius, his other son, did little better; who died indeed of sickness, but after that Julianus had taken arms against him.* The destruction of Demetrius, son to Philip the Second of Macedon, turned upon the father, who died of repentance.† And many like examples there are, but few or none where the fathers had good by such distrust; except it were where the sons were up in open arms against them, as was Selymus the First against Bajazet, and the three sons of Henry the Second, King of England.

For their prelates: when they are proud and great, there

---

* Constantine the Great, Roman emperor 306–37, executed his son Crispus in 326. At Constantine's death, the empire was divided between his sons: Constantine II was killed while attempting to overthrow his brother Constans (whom Bacon calls Constance); Constans himself was murdered in his bed by his own men; and Constantius died in 361 on his way to oppose Julian, who had been proclaimed emperor by his troops.

† Demetrius, son of Philip V of Macedon, was falsely accused of treason by his brother, the crown-prince Perseus. His father had him put to death in 179 BC. Bacon has confused Philip V with Philip II, father of Alexander the Great.

is also danger from them. As it was in the times of Anselmus and Thomas Becket, archbishops of Canterbury, who with their crosiers did almost try it with the king's sword; and yet they had to deal with stout and haughty kings, William Rufus, Henry the First, and Henry the Second.* The danger is not from that state but where it hath a dependence of foreign authority, or where the churchmen come in and are elected, not by the collation of the king or particular patrons, but by the people.

For their nobles: to keep them at a distance, it is not amiss; but to depress them may make a king more absolute, but less safe, and less able to perform anything that he desires. I have noted it in my history of King Henry the Seventh of England, who depressed his nobility; whereupon it came to pass that his times were full of difficulties and troubles, for the nobility, though they continued loyal unto him, yet did they not co-operate with him in his business. So that in effect he was fain to do all things himself.

For their second-nobles: there is not much danger from them, being a body dispersed. They may sometimes discourse high, but that doth little hurt; besides, they are a counterpoise to the higher nobility, that they grow not too potent; and lastly, being the most immediate in authority with the common people, they do best temper popular commotions.

* Anselm, d. 1109, was twice sent into exile for asserting the rights of the clergy against the secular authority of William Rufus and Henry I. Thomas à Becket was murdered in Canterbury Cathedral in 1170 after violent disputes with Henry II.

For their merchants: they are *vena porta* [the gate vein], and if they flourish not, a kingdom may have good limbs, but will have empty veins and nourish little. Taxes and imposts upon them do seldom good to the king's revenue, for that that he wins in the hundred,* he loseth in the shire, the particular rates being increased, but the total bulk of trading rather decreased.

For their commons: there is little danger from them, except it be where they have great and potent heads, or where you meddle with the point of religion or their customs or means of life.

For their men of war: it is a dangerous state where they live and remain in a body, and are used to donatives; whereof we see examples in the janizaries,† and Praetorian bands‡ of Rome. But trainings of men, and arming them in several places, and under several commanders, and without donatives, are things of defence, and no danger.

Princes are like to heavenly bodies, which cause good or evil times, and which have much veneration, but no rest. All precepts concerning kings are in effect comprehended in those two remembrances: *Memento quod es homo*, and *Memento quod es Deus*, or *vice Dei* [Remember that you are a man and remember that you are a god, or God's viceregent]: the one bridleth their power, and the other their will.

---

* A subdivision of the shire.
† Bodyguards to the Turkish sultans.
‡ Bodyguards to the Roman emperors.

Of Cunning

We take cunning for a sinister or crooked wisdom. And certainly there is great difference between a cunning man and a wise man, not only in point of honesty, but in point of ability. There be that can pack the cards, and yet cannot play well; so there are some that are good in canvasses and factions, that are otherwise weak men. Again, it is one thing to understand persons, and another thing to understand matters: for many are perfect in men's humours, that are not greatly capable of the real part of business, which is the constitution of one that hath studied men more than books. Such men are fitter for practice than for counsel, and they are good but in their own alley: turn them to new men, and they have lost their aim; so as the old rule to know a fool from a wise man, *Mitte ambos nudos ad ignotos et videbis* [Send both of them naked among strangers and then you will see],* doth scarce hold for them. And because these cunning men are like haberdashers of small wares, it is not amiss to set forth their shop.

It is a point of cunning to wait upon him with whom you speak, with your eye, as the Jesuits give it in precept;

* Attributed to Aristippus in Diogenes Laertius, *Lives of Eminent Philosophers*, II.73.

for there be many wise men that have secret hearts and transparent countenances. Yet this would be done with a demure abasing of your eye sometimes, as the Jesuits also do use.

Another is that when you have anything to obtain of present dispatch, you entertain and amuse the party with whom you deal with some other discourse, that he be not too much awake to make objections. I knew a counsellor and secretary that never came to Queen Elizabeth of England with bills to sign, but he would always first put her into some discourse of estate, that she mought the less mind the bills.

The like surprise may be made by moving things when the party is in haste and cannot stay to consider advisedly of that is moved.

If a man would cross a business that he doubts some other would handsomely and effectually move, let him pretend to wish it well, and move it himself in such sort as may foil it.

The breaking off in the midst of that one was about to say, as if he took himself up, breeds a greater appetite in him with whom you confer, to know more.

And because it works better when anything seemeth to be gotten from you by question than if you offer it of yourself, you may lay a bait for a question by showing another visage and countenance than you are wont; to the end to give occasion for the party to ask what the matter is of the change [. . .]

In things that are tender and unpleasing, it is good to break the ice by some whose words are of less weight, and to reserve the more weighty voice to come in as by chance, so that he may be asked the question upon the other's speech [. . .]

In things that a man would not be seen in himself, it is a point of cunning to borrow the name of the world; as to say, *The world says*, or, *There is a speech abroad*.

I knew one that, when he wrote a letter, he would put that which was most material in the postscript, as if it had been a by-matter.

I knew another that, when he came to have speech, he would pass over that that he intended most, and go forth, and come back again and speak of it as of a thing that he had almost forgot.

Some procure themselves to be surprised at such times as it is like the party that they work upon will suddenly come upon them, and to be found with a letter in their hand, or doing somewhat which they are not accustomed; to the end they may be apposed of those things which of themselves they are desirous to utter.

It is a point of cunning to let fall those words in a man's own name, which he would have another man learn and use, and thereupon take advantage. I knew two that were competitors for the secretary's place in Queen Elizabeth's time, and yet kept good quarter between themselves, and would confer one with another upon the business; and the one of them said that to be a secretary in the *declination of a monarchy* was a ticklish thing, and that he did not affect it. The other straight caught up those words and discoursed with divers of his friends that he had no reason to desire to be secretary in the *declination of a monarchy*. The first man took hold of it and found means it was told the Queen; who, hearing of *a declination of a monarchy*, took it so ill as she would never after hear of the other's suit.

There is a cunning, which we in England call *The turning of the cat in the pan*, which is, when that which a man says to another, he lays it as if another had said it to him. And to say truth, it is not easy, when such a matter passed between two, to make it appear from which of them it first moved and began [. . .]

Some have in readiness so many tales and stories, as there is nothing they would insinuate but they can wrap it into a tale, which serveth both to keep themselves more in guard and to make others carry it with more pleasure.

It is a good point of cunning for a man to shape the answer he would have, in his own words and propositions, for it makes the other party stick the less.

It is strange how long some men will lie in wait to speak somewhat they desire to say, and how far about they will fetch, and how many other matters they will beat over to come near it. It is a thing of great patience, but yet of much use.

A sudden, bold, and unexpected question doth many times surprise a man, and lay him open. Like to him, that having changed his name, and walking in Paul's, another suddenly came behind him and called him by his true name, whereat straightways he looked back.

But these small wares and petty points of cunning are infinite, and it were a good deed to make a list of them, for that nothing doth more hurt in a state than that cunning men pass for wise.

But certainly some there are that know the resorts and falls of business, that cannot sink into the main of it; like a house that hath convenient stairs and entries but never a fair room. Therefore you shall see them find out pretty looses in the conclusion, but are no ways able to examine or debate matters. And yet commonly they take advantage of their inability, and would be thought wits of direction. Some build rather upon the abusing of others, and (as we now say) *putting tricks upon them*, than upon soundness of their own proceedings. But Solomon saith: *Prudens advertit ad gressus suos; stultus divertit ad dolos* [The wise man pays attention to the steps he is taking: the fool turns aside to the snares].*

* Derived from Proverbs 14.8 and 15.

Of Wisdom for a Man's Self

An ant is a wise creature for itself, but it is a shrewd thing in an orchard or garden. And certainly men that are great lovers of themselves waste the public. Divide with reason between self-love and society, and be so true to thyself as thou be not false to others, specially to thy king and country. It is a poor centre of a man's actions, *himself*. It is right earth, for that only stands fast upon his own centre, whereas all things that have affinity with the heavens move upon the centre of another, which they benefit. The referring of all to a man's self is more tolerable in a sovereign prince, because themselves are not only themselves, but their good and evil is at the peril of the public fortune. But it is a desperate evil in a servant to a prince, or a citizen in a republic. For whatsoever affairs pass such a man's hands, he crooketh them to his own ends; which must needs be often eccentric to the ends of his master or state. Therefore let princes or states choose such servants as have not this mark, except they mean their service should be made but the accessary. That which maketh the effect more pernicious is that all proportion is lost. It were disproportion enough for the servant's good to be preferred before the master's, but yet it is a greater extreme when a little good of the servant shall carry things against a great good of the master's. And yet that is the case of bad officers, treasurers,

ambassadors, generals, and other false and corrupt servants, which set a bias upon their bowl, of their own
petty ends and envies, to the overthrow of their master's
great and important affairs. And for the most part, the
good such servants receive is after the model of their
own fortune, but the hurt they sell for that good is after
the model of their master's fortune. And certainly it is
the nature of extreme self-lovers, as they will set an
house on fire, and it were but to roast their eggs. And
yet these men many times hold credit with their masters,
because their study is but to please them and profit
themselves; and for either respect they will abandon the
good of their affairs.

Wisdom for a man's self is, in many branches thereof,
a depraved thing. It is the wisdom of rats, that will be
sure to leave a house somewhat before it fall. It is the
wisdom of the fox, that thrusts out the badger, who
digged and made room for him. It is the wisdom of
crocodiles, that shed tears when they would devour. But
that which is specially to be noted is, that those which
(as Cicero says of Pompey) are *sui amantes sine rivali*
[lovers of themselves without rivals],* are many times
unfortunate. And whereas they have all their time sacri-
ficed to themselves, they become in the end themselves
sacrifices to the inconstancy of fortune, whose wings
they thought by their self-wisdom to have pinioned.

* From *Letters to his Brother Quintus*, III.8.

Of Innovations

As the births of living creatures at first are ill-shapen, so are all innovations, which are the births of time. Yet notwithstanding, as those that first bring honour into their family are commonly more worthy than most that succeed, so the first precedent (if it be good) is seldom attained by imitation. For ill, to man's nature as it stands perverted, hath a natural motion, strongest in continuance; but good, as a forced motion, strongest at first. Surely ever medicine is an innovation, and he that will not apply new remedies must expect new evils. For time is the greatest innovator, and if time of course alter things to the worse, and wisdom and counsel shall not alter them to the better, what shall be the end? It is true that what is settled by custom, though it be not good, yet at least it is fit. And those things which have long gone together are as it were confederate within themselves: whereas new things piece not so well, but though they help by their utility, yet they trouble by their inconformity. Besides, they are like strangers, more admired and less favoured. All this is true, if time stood still, which contrariwise moveth so round that a froward retention of custom is as turbulent a thing as an innovation; and they that reverence too much old times are but a scorn to the new. It were good therefore that men in their innovations would follow the example of time itself, which indeed innovateth greatly, but quietly and by degrees scarce to be perceived. For otherwise, whatsoever is new is unlooked for, and ever it mends some, and pairs other: and he that is holpen takes it for a fortune, and thanks the time; and he that is hurt, for a wrong, and imputeth it to the author. It is good also not to try experiments in states, except the necessity be urgent or the utility evident; and well to beware that it be the reformation that draweth on the change, and not the desire of change that pretendeth the reformation. And lastly, that the novelty, though it be not rejected, yet be held for a suspect, and, as the Scripture saith, *that we make a stand upon the ancient way, and then look about us, and discover what is the straight and right way, and so to walk in it.**

Of Expense

Riches are for spending; and spending for honour and good actions. Therefore extraordinary expense must be limited by the worth of the occasion, for voluntary undoing may be as well for a man's country as for the kingdom of heaven. But ordinary expense ought to be limited by a man's estate, and governed with such regard, as it be within his compass, and not subject to deceit and abuse of servants, and ordered to the best show, that the bills may be less than the estimation abroad. Certainly if a man will keep but of even hand, his ordinary expenses ought to be but to the half of his receipts; and if he think to wax rich, but to the third part. It is no baseness for the greatest to descend and look into their own estate. Some forbear it, not upon negligence alone, but doubting to bring themselves into melancholy, in respect they shall find it broken. But wounds cannot be cured without searching. He that cannot look into his own estate at all, had need both choose well those whom he employeth, and change them often; for new are more timorous and less subtle. He that can look into his estate but seldom, it behoveth him to turn all to certainties. A man had need, if he be plentiful in some kind of expense, to be as saving again in some other. As, if he be plentiful in diet, to be saving in apparel; if he be plentiful in the hall, to be saving in the stable; and the like. For he that is plentiful in expenses of all kinds will hardly be preserved from decay. In clearing of a man's estate, he may as well hurt himself in being too sudden, as in letting it run on too long. For hasty selling is commonly as disadvantageable as interest. Besides, he that clears at once will relapse, for, finding himself out of straits, he will revert to his customs: but he that cleareth by degrees induceth a habit of frugality, and gaineth as well upon his mind as upon his estate.

Certainly, who hath a state to repair may not despise small things, and commonly it is less dishonourable to abridge petty charges than to stoop to petty gettings. A man ought warily to begin charges which once begun will continue; but in matters that return not he may be more magnificent.

Of Regiment of Health

There is a wisdom in this beyond the rules of physic: a man's own observation, what he finds good of, and what he finds hurt of, is the best physic to preserve health. But it is a safer conclusion to say, *This agreeth not well with me, therefore I will not continue it*, than this, *I find no offence of this, therefore I may use it*. For strength of nature in youth passeth over many excesses which are owing a man till his age. Discern of the coming on of years, and think not to do the same things still; for age will not be defied. Beware of sudden change in any great point of diet, and if necessity enforce it, fit the rest to it. For it is a secret, both in nature and state, that it is safer to change many things than one. Examine thy customs of diet, sleep, exercise, apparel and the like, and try in anything thou shalt judge hurtful, to discontinue it by little and little; but so as if thou dost find any inconvenience by the change, thou come back to it again: for it is hard to distinguish that which is generally held good and wholesome from that which is good particularly and fit for thine own body. To be free-minded and cheerfully disposed at hours of meat and of sleep and of exercise, is one of the best precepts of long lasting. As for the passions and studies of the mind, avoid envy, anxious fears, anger fretting inwards, subtle and knotty inquisitions, joys and exhilarations in excess, sadness not communicated. Entertain hopes, mirth rather than joy, variety of delights rather than surfeit of them, wonder and admiration (and therefore novelties), studies that fill the mind with splendid and illustrious objects (as histories, fables, and contemplations of nature). If you fly physic in health altogether, it will be too strange for your body when you shall need it. If you make it too familiar, it will work no extraordinary effect when sickness cometh. I commend rather some diet for certain seasons than frequent use of physic, except it be grown into a custom: for those diets alter the body more, and trouble it less. Despise no new accident in your body, but ask opinion of it. In sickness, respect health principally; and in health, action. For those that put their bodies to endure in health may, in most sicknesses which are not very sharp, be cured only with diet and tendering. Celsus could never have spoken it as a physician, had he not been a wise man withal, when he giveth it for one of the great precepts of health and lasting, that a man do vary and interchange contraries, but with an inclination to the more benign extreme: use fasting and full eating, but rather full eating; watching and sleep, but rather sleep; sitting and exercise, but rather exercise; and the like. So shall nature be cherished and yet taught masteries. Physicians are some of them so pleasing and conformable to the humour of the patient, as they press not the true cure of the disease; and some other are so regular in proceeding according to art for the disease, as they respect not sufficiently the condition of the patient. Take one of a middle temper; or, if it may not be found in one man, combine two of either sort; and forget not to call as well the best acquainted with your body, as the best reputed of for his faculty.

Of Suspicion

Suspicions amongst thoughts are like bats amongst birds:
they ever fly by twilight. Certainly they are to be repressed, or at the least well guarded, for they cloud the
mind, they leese friends, and they check with business,
whereby business cannot go on currently and constantly.
They dispose kings to tyranny, husbands to jealousy,
wise men to irresolution and melancholy. They are
defects, not in the heart but in the brain, for they take
place in the stoutest natures, as in the example of Henry
the Seventh of England. There was not a more suspicious
man, nor a more stout. And in such a composition they
do small hurt, for commonly they are not admitted but
with examination whether they be likely or no: but in
fearful natures they gain ground too fast. There is nothing makes a man suspect much, more than to know
little; and therefore men should remedy suspicion by
procuring to know more, and not to keep their suspicions
in smother. What would men have? Do they think those
they employ and deal with are saints? Do they not think
they will have their own ends, and be truer to themselves
than to them? Therefore there is no better way to moderate suspicions than to account upon such suspicions as
true and yet to bridle them as false. For so far a man
ought to make use of suspicions, as to provide as, if that
should be true that he suspects, yet it may do him no

hurt. Suspicions that the mind of itself gathers are but buzzes, but suspicions that are artificially nourished and put into men's heads by the tales and whisperings of others, have stings. Certainly the best mean to clear the way in this same wood of suspicions is frankly to communicate them with the party that he suspects: for thereby he shall be sure to know more of the truth of them than he did before, and withal shall make that party more circumspect not to give further cause of suspicion. But this would not be done to men of base natures, for they, if they find themselves once suspected, will never be true. The Italian says, *Sospetto licentia fede* [suspicion permits fidelity to depart], as if suspicion did give a passport to faith; but it ought rather to kindle it to discharge itself.

Of Discourse

Some in their discourse desire rather commendation of
wit, in being able to hold all arguments, than of judgement, in discerning what is true; as if it were a praise
to know what might be said, and not what should be
thought. Some have certain commonplaces and themes
wherein they are good, and want variety; which kind of
poverty is for the most part tedious, and, when it is once
perceived, ridiculous. The honourablest part of talk is to
give the occasion, and again to moderate and pass to
somewhat else, for then a man leads the dance. It is
good, in discourse and speech of conversation, to vary
and intermingle speech of the present occasion with
arguments, tales with reasons, asking of questions with
telling of opinions, and jest with earnest: for it is a dull
thing to tire, and, as we say now, to jade anything too
far. As for jest, there be certain things which ought to be
privileged from it; namely, religion, matters of state,
great persons, any man's present business of importance,
and any case that deserveth pity. Yet there be some that
think their wits have been asleep, except they dart out
somewhat that is piquant and to the quick. That is a vein
which would be bridled:

Parce, puer, stimulis, et fortius utere loris.
[Spare the whip, boy, and pull harder on the reins]*

And generally, men ought to find the difference between
saltness and bitterness. Certainly he that hath a satirical
vein, as he maketh others afraid of his wit, so he had
need be afraid of others' memory. He that questioneth
much shall learn much and content much, but especially
if he apply his questions to the skill of the persons whom
he asketh; for he shall give them occasion to please
themselves in speaking, and himself shall continually
gather knowledge. But let his questions not be trouble-
some, for that is fit for a poser. And let him be sure to
leave other men their turns to speak. Nay, if there be
any that would reign and take up all the time, let him
find means to take them off and to bring others on, as
musicians use to do with those that dance too long
galliards. If you dissemble sometimes your knowledge
of that you are thought to know, you shall be thought
another time to know that you know not. Speech of a
man's self ought to be seldom and well chosen. I knew
one was wont to say in scorn, *He must needs be a wise
man, he speaks so much of himself*. And there is but one
case wherein a man may commend himself with good
grace, and that is in commending virtue in another,
especially if it be such a virtue whereunto himself pretendeth. Speech of touch towards others should be sparingly
used, for discourse ought to be as a field, without coming
home to any man. I knew two noblemen, of the west

* Ovid, *Metamorphoses*, II.127.

part of England, whereof the one was given to scoff, but kept ever royal cheer in his house; the other would ask of those that had been at the other's table, *Tell truly, was there never a flout or dry blow* given?* To which the guest would answer, *Such and such a thing passed.* The lord would say, *I thought he would mar a good dinner.* Discretion of speech is more than eloquence, and to speak agreeably to him with whom we deal is more than to speak in good words or in good order. A good continued speech, without a good speech of interlocution, shows slowness; and a good reply or second speech, without a good settled speech, showeth shallowness and weakness. As we see in beasts, that those that are weakest in the course are yet nimblest in the turn, as it is betwixt the greyhound and the hare. To use too many circumstances ere one come to the matter is wearisome; to use none at all is blunt.

---

* A jibe or sarcastic comment.

Of Riches

I cannot call riches better than the baggage of virtue. The Roman word is better, *impedimenta*. For as the baggage is to an army, so is riches to virtue. It cannot be spared nor left behind, but it hindereth the march; yea, and the care of it sometimes loseth or disturbeth the victory. Of great riches there is no real use, except it be in the distribution; the rest is but conceit. So saith Solomon, *Where much is, there are many to consume it; and what hath the owner but the sight of it with his eyes?** The personal fruition in any man cannot reach to feel great riches: there is a custody of them, or a power of dole and donative of them, or a fame of them; but no solid use to the owner. Do you not see what feigned prices are set upon little stones and rarities, and what works of ostentation are undertaken, because there might seem to be some use of great riches? But then you will say, they may be of use to buy men out of dangers or troubles. As Solomon saith, *Riches are as a stronghold in the imagination of the rich man.*† But this is excellently expressed, that it is in imagination, and not always in fact. For certainly great riches have sold more men than they have bought out. Seek not proud riches, but such as thou mayest get justly, use soberly, distribute cheerfully,

* Ecclesiastes 5.11. †Proverbs 18.11.

and leave contentedly. Yet have no abstract nor friarly contempt of them. But distinguish, as Cicero saith well of Rabirius Postumus: *In studio rei amplificandae apparebat non avaritiae praedam sed instrumentum bonitati quaert* [In his keeness to increase his wealth it was apparent that he was not seeking a prey for avarice to feed upon, but an instrument for good to work with].* Hearken also to Solomon, and beware of hasty gathering of riches: *Qui festinat ad divitias, non erit insons* [He who makes haste to be rich shall not be innocent].† The poets feign that when Plutus (which is riches) is sent from Jupiter, he limps and goes slowly, but when he is sent from Pluto, he runs and is swift of foot: meaning, that riches gotten by good means and just labour pace slowly, but when they come by the death of others (as by the course of inheritance, testaments, and the like), they come tumbling upon a man. But it mought be applied likewise to Pluto, taking him for the devil. For when riches come from the devil (as by fraud and oppression and unjust means), they come upon speed. The ways to enrich are many, and most of them foul. Parsimony is one of the best, and yet is not innocent, for it withholdeth men from works of liberality and charity. The improvement of the ground is the most natural obtaining of riches, for it is our great mother's blessing, the earth's; but it is slow. And yet where men of great wealth do stoop to husbandry, it multiplieth riches exceedingly. I knew a nobleman in

* *The Speech on behalf of Rabirius Postumus*, II. Cicero is not speaking of Rabirius Postumus, but his father, Gaius Curtius.
† Proverbs 28.20.

England, that had the greatest audits of any man in my time: a great grazier, a great sheep-master, a great timber-man, a great collier, a great corn-master, a great lead-man, and so of iron, and a number of the like points of husbandry: so as the earth seemed a sea to him, in respect of the perpetual importation. It was truly observed by one, that himself came very hardly to a little riches, and very easily to great riches. For when a man's stock is come to that, that he can expect the prime of markets, and overcome those bargains which for their greatness are few men's money, and be partner in the industries of younger men, he cannot but increase mainly. The gains of ordinary trades and vocations are honest, and furthered by two things chiefly: by diligence, and by a good name for good and fair dealing. But the gains of bargains are of a more doubtful nature, when men shall wait upon others' necessity, broke by servants and instruments to draw them on, put off others cunningly that would be better chapmen, and the like practices, which are crafty and naught. As for the chopping of bargains, when a man buys not to hold, but to sell over again, that commonly grindeth double, both upon the seller and upon the buyer. Sharings do greatly enrich, if the hands be well chosen that are trusted. Usury is the certainest means of gain, though one of the worst, as that whereby a man doth eat his bread *in sudore vultus alieni* [in the sweat of another man's brow];* and besides, doth plough upon Sundays. But yet certain though it be, it hath flaws, for that the scriveners and brokers do value

* See Genesis 3.19.

unsound men to serve their own turn. The fortune in being the first in an invention or in a privilege doth cause sometimes a wonderful overgrowth in riches, as it was with the first sugar man in the Canaries. Therefore if a man can play the true logician, to have as well judgement as invention, he may do great matters, especially if the times be fit. He that resteth upon gains certain shall hardly grow to great riches, and he that puts all upon adventures doth oftentimes break and come to poverty: it is good therefore to guard adventures with certainties that may uphold losses. Monopolies and coemption of wares for re-sale, where they are not restrained, are great means to enrich, especially if the party have intelligence what things are like to come into request, and so store himself beforehand. Riches gotten by service, though it be of the best rise, yet when they are gotten by flattery, feeding humours, and other servile conditions, they may be placed amongst the worst. As for fishing for testaments and executorships (as Tacitus saith of Seneca, *testamenta et orbos tanquam indagine capi* [he seized wills and wardships as with a net]*), it is yet worse, by how much men submit themselves to meaner persons than in service. Believe not much them that seem to despise riches, for they despise them that despair of them; and none worse when they come to them. Be not penny-wise; riches have wings, and sometimes they fly away of themselves, sometimes they must be set flying to bring in more. Men leave their riches either to their kindred, or to the public, and moderate portions prosper best in

---

* *Annals*, XIII.42.

both. A great state left to an heir is as a lure to all the birds of prey round about to seize on him, if he be not the better stablished in years and judgement. Likewise glorious gifts and foundations are like *sacrifices without salt*, and but the painted sepulchres of alms, which soon will putrefy and corrupt inwardly. Therefore measure not thine advancements by quantity, but frame them by measure: and defer not charities till death, for certainly if a man weigh it rightly, he that doth so is rather liberal of another man's than of his own.

Of Ambition

Ambition is like choler, which is an humour that maketh men active, earnest, full of alacrity, and stirring, if it be not stopped. But if it be stopped, and cannot have his way, it becometh adust, and thereby malign and venomous. So ambitious men, if they find the way open for their rising, and still get forward, they are rather busy than dangerous; but if they be checked in their desires, they become secretly discontent and look upon men and matters with an evil eye, and are best pleased when things go backward, which is the worst property in a servant of a prince or state. Therefore it is good for princes, if they use ambitious men, to handle it so as they be still progressive and not retrograde; which because it cannot be without inconvenience, it is good not to use such natures at all. For if they rise not with their service, they will take order to make their service fall with them. But since we have said it were good not to use men of ambitious natures, except it be upon necessity, it is fit we speak in what cases they are of necessity. Good commanders in the wars must be taken, be they never so ambitious; for the use of their service dispenseth with the rest, and to take a soldier without ambition is to pull off his spurs. There is also great use of ambitious men in being screens to princes in matters of danger and envy, for no man will take that part, except he be like a seeled dove, that mounts and mounts because he cannot see about him. There is use also of ambitious men in pulling down the greatness of any subject that overtops [. . .] Since therefore they must be used in such cases, there resteth to speak how they are to be bridled that they may be less dangerous. There is less danger of them if they be of mean birth, than if they be noble; and if they be rather harsh of nature, than gracious and popular; and if they be rather new raised, than grown cunning and fortified in their greatness. It is counted by some a weakness in princes to have favourites, but it is of all others the best remedy against ambitious great ones. For when the way of pleasuring and displeasuring lieth by the favourite, it is impossible any other should be over-great. Another means to curb them is to balance them by others as proud as they. But then there must be some middle counsellors to keep things steady, for without that ballast the ship will roll too much. At the least, a prince may animate and inure some meaner persons to be as it were scourges to ambitious men. As for the having of them obnoxious to ruin, if they be of fearful natures, it may do well, but if they be stout and daring, it may precipitate their designs and prove dangerous. As for the pulling of them down, if the affairs require it, and that it may not be done with safety suddenly, the only way is the interchange continually of favours and disgraces, whereby they may not know what to expect, and be as it were in a wood. Of ambitions, it is less harmful, the ambition to prevail in great things, than that other, to appear in everything, for that breeds confusion, and mars business. But yet it is less danger to have an ambitious man stirring in business, than great in dependences. He that seeketh to be eminent amongst able men hath a great task, but that is ever good for the public. But he that plots to be the only figure amongst ciphers is the decay of an whole age. Honour hath three things in it: the vantage ground to do good, the approach to kings and principal persons, and the raising of a man's own fortunes. He that hath the best of these intentions, when he aspireth, is an honest man; and that prince that can discern of these intentions in another that aspireth, is a wise prince. Generally let princes and states choose such ministers as are more sensible of duty than of rising; and such as love business rather upon conscience than upon bravery; and let them discern a busy nature from a willing mind.

Of Beauty

Virtue is like a rich stone, best plain set: and surely virtue is best in a body that is comely, though not of delicate features, and that hath rather dignity of presence than beauty of aspect. Neither is it almost seen, that very beautiful persons are otherwise of great virtue, as if nature were rather busy not to err, than in labour to produce excellency. And therefore they prove accomplished, but not of great spirit, and study rather behaviour than virtue. But this holds not always; for Augustus Caesar, Titus Vespasianus, Philip le Bel of France, Edward the Fourth of England, Alcibiades of Athens, Ismael the Sophy of Persia, were all high and great spirits, and yet the most beautiful men of their times. In beauty, that of favour is more than that of colour, and that of decent and gracious motion more than that of favour. That is the best part of beauty which a picture cannot express; no, nor the first sight of the life. There is no excellent beauty that hath not some strangeness in the proportion. A man cannot tell whether Apelles* or Albert Dürer were the more trifler; whereof the one would make a personage by geometrical proportions, the other, by taking the best parts out of divers faces to make one excellent. Such personages, I think, would please nobody

* Greek painter, fourth century BC.

but the painter that made them. Not but I think a painter may make a better face then ever was, but he must do it by a kind of felicity (as a musician that maketh an excellent air in music), and not by rule. A man shall see faces that, if you examine them part by part, you shall find never a good, and yet all together do well. If it be true that the principal part of beauty is in decent motion, certainly it is no marvel though persons in years seem many times more amiable: *pulchrorum autumnus pulcher* [the autumn of the beautiful is beautiful];* for no youth can be comely but by pardon, and considering the youth as to make up the comeliness. Beauty is as summer fruits, which are easy to corrupt, and cannot last; and for the most part it makes a dissolute youth, and an age a little out of countenance: but yet certainly again, if it light well, it maketh virtues shine, and vices blush.

* A saying of Euripides, preserved in Plutarch, *Alcibiades*, I.3.

Of Deformity

Deformed persons are commonly even with nature: for as nature hath done ill by them, so do they by nature, being for the most part (as the Scripture saith) *void of natural affection* and so they have their revenge of nature. Certainly there is a consent between the body and the mind, and *where nature erreth in the one, she ventureth in the other: Ubi peccat in uno, periclitatur in altero* [While she errs in the one, she runs a risk in the other]. But because there is in man an election touching the frame of his mind, and a necessity in the frame of his body, the stars of natural inclination are sometimes obscured by the sun of discipline and virtue. Therefore it is good to consider of deformity, not as a sign, which is more deceivable, but as a cause, which seldom faileth of the effect. Whosoever hath anything fixed in his person that doth induce contempt, hath also a perpetual spur in himself to rescue and deliver himself from scorn. Therefore all deformed persons are extreme bold – first, as in their own defence, as being exposed to scorn, but in process of time, by a general habit. Also, it stirreth in them industry, and especially of this kind, to watch and observe the weakness of others, that they may have somewhat to repay. Again, in their superiors, it quencheth jealousy towards them, as persons that they think they may at pleasure despise; and it layeth their competitors and emulators asleep, as never believing they should be in possibility of advancement, till they see them in possession. So that upon the matter, in a great wit deformity is an advantage to rising. Kings in ancient times (and at this present in some countries) were wont to put great trust in eunuchs, because they that are envious towards all are more obnoxious and officious towards one. But yet their trust towards them hath rather been as to good spials and good whisperers than good magistrates and officers. And much like is the reason of deformed persons. Still the ground is, they will, if they be of spirit, seek to free themselves from scorn, which must be either by virtue or malice. And therefore let it not be marvelled if sometimes they prove excellent persons; as was Agesilaus, Zanger the son of Solyman, Aesop, Gasca, President of Peru; and Socrates may go likewise amongst them, with others.

Of Building

Houses are built to live in, and not to look on; therefore let use be preferred before uniformity, except where both may be had. Leave the goodly fabrics of houses, for beauty only, to the enchanted palaces of the poets; who build them with small cost. He that builds a fair house upon an ill seat, committeth himself to prison. Neither do I reckon it an ill seat only where the air is unwholesome, but likewise where the air is unequal. As you shall see many fine seats set upon a knap of ground, environed with higher hills round about it, whereby the heat of the sun is pent in and the wind gathereth as in troughs; so as you shall have, and that suddenly, as great diversity of heat and cold as if you dwelt in several places. Neither is it ill air only that maketh an ill seat, but ill ways, ill markets, and (if you will consult with Momus) ill neighbours. I speak not of many more: want of water; want of wood, shade, and shelter; want of fruitfulness, and mixture of grounds of several natures; want of prospect; want of level grounds; want of places at some near distance for sports of hunting, hawking, and races; too near the sea, too remote; having the commodity of navigable rivers, or the discommodity of their overflowing; too far off from great cities, which may hinder business, or too near them, which lurcheth all provisions, and maketh everything dear; where a man hath a great living laid together, and where he is scanted. All which, as it is impossible perhaps to find together, so it is good to know them and think of them, that a man may take as many as he can, and, if he have several dwellings, that he sort them so, that what he wanteth in the one he may find in the other. Lucullus answered Pompey well, who, when he saw his stately galleries and rooms so large and lightsome in one of his houses, said, *Surely an excellent place for summer, but how do you in winter?* Lucullus answered, *Why, do you not think me as wise as some fowl are, that ever change their abode towards the winter?*

To pass from the seat to the house itself; we will do as Cicero doth in the orator's art, who writes books *De Oratore*, and a book he entitles *Orator*, whereof the former delivers the precepts of the art, and the latter the perfection. We will therefore describe a princely palace, making a brief model thereof. For it is strange to see, now in Europe, such huge buildings as the Vatican and Escurial and some others be, and yet scarce a very fair room in them.

First, therefore, I say you cannot have a perfect palace except you have two several sides: a side for the banquet, as is spoken of in the book of Hester, and a side for the household; the one for feasts and triumphs, and the other for dwelling. I understand both these sides to be not only returns, but parts of the front, and to be uniform without, though severally partitioned within; and to be on both sides of a great and stately tower in the midst of the front, that, as it were, joineth them together on either hand. I would have on the side of the banquet, in front, one only goodly room above stairs, of some forty foot high, and under it a room for a dressing or preparing place at times of triumphs. On the other side, which is the household side, I wish it divided at the first into a hall and a chapel (with a partition between), both of good state and bigness; and those not to go all the length, but to have at the further end a winter and a summer parlour, both fair. And under these rooms, a fair and large cellar, sunk under ground, and likewise some privy kitchens, with butteries and pantries, and the like. As for the tower, I would have it two stories, of eighteen foot high apiece, above the two wings; and a goodly leads upon the top railed with statuas interposed; and the same tower to be divided into rooms, as shall be thought fit. The stairs likewise to the upper rooms; let them be upon a fair open newel, and finely railed in with images of wood cast into a brass colour; and a very fair landing place at the top. But this to be, if you do not point any of the lower rooms for a dining place of servants. For otherwise you shall have the servants' dinner after your own: for the steam of it will come up as in a tunnel. And so much for the front. Only, I understand the height of the first stairs to be sixteen foot, which is the height of the lower room.

Beyond this front is there to be a fair court, but three sides of it of a far lower building than the front. And in all the four corners of that court, fair staircases, cast into turrets on the outside, and not within the row of buildings themselves. But those towers are not to be of the height of the front, but rather proportionable to the lower building. Let the court not be paved, for that striketh up a great heat in summer and much cold in winter. But only some side alleys, with a cross, and the quarters to graze, being kept shorn, but not too near shorn. The row of return, on the banquet side, let it be all stately galleries, in which galleries let there be three or five fine cupolas in the length of it, placed at equal distance, and fine coloured windows of several works. On the household side, chambers of presence and ordinary entertainments, with some bedchambers; and let all three sides be a double house, without thorough-lights on the sides, that you may have rooms from the sun, both for forenoon and afternoon. Cast it also that you may have rooms both for summer and winter, shady for summer, and warm for winter. You shall have sometimes fair houses so full of glass that one cannot tell where to become to be out of the sun or cold. For inbowed windows, I hold them of good use (in cities, indeed, upright do better, in respect of the uniformity towards the street), for they be pretty retiring places for conference; and besides, they keep both the wind and sun off, for that which would strike almost thorough the room doth scarce pass the window. But let them be but few, four in the court, on the sides only.

Beyond this court, let there be an inward court of the same square and height, which is to be environed with the garden on all sides; and in the inside, cloistered on all sides, upon decent and beautiful arches, as high as the first storey. On the under storey, towards the garden, let it be turned to a grotta, or place of shade or estivation; and only have opening and windows towards the garden; and be level upon the floor, no whit sunk under ground, to avoid all dampishness. And let there be a fountain, or some fair work of statuas, in the midst of this court; and to be paved as the other court was. These buildings to be for privy lodgings on both sides, and the end for privy galleries. Whereof you must foresee that one of them be for an infirmary, if the prince or any special person should be sick, with chambers, bedchamber, antecamera, and recamera joining to it. This upon the second storey. Upon the ground storey, a fair gallery, open, upon pillars; and upon the third storey likewise, an open gallery upon pillars, to take the prospect and freshness of the garden. At both corners of the further side, by way of return, let there be two delicate or rich cabinets, daintily paved, richly hanged, glazed with crystalline glass, and a rich cupola in the midst; and all other elegancy that may be thought upon. In the upper gallery too, I wish that there may be, if the place will yield it, some fountains running in divers places from the wall, with some fine avoidances. And thus much for the model of the palace, save that you must have, before you come to the front, three courts. A green court plain, with a wall about it; a second court of the same, but more garnished, with little turrets, or rather embellishments, upon the wall; and a third court, to make a square with the front, but not to be built, nor yet enclosed with a naked wall, but enclosed with terraces, leaded aloft, and fairly garnished, on the three sides; and cloistered on the inside, with pillars and not with arches below. As for offices, let them stand at distance, with some low galleries, to pass from them to the palace itself.

Of Gardens

God Almighty first planted a garden. And indeed it is the purest of human pleasures. It is the greatest refreshment to the spirits of man, without which buildings and palaces are but gross handyworks: and a man shall ever see that when ages grow to civility and elegancy, men come to build stately sooner than to garden finely, as if gardening were the greater perfection. I do hold it, in the royal ordering of gardens, there ought to be gardens for all the months in the year, in which severally things of beauty may be then in season. For December and January and the latter part of November, you must take such things as are green all winter: holly, ivy, bays, juniper, cypress-trees, yew, pineapple-trees; fir-trees; rosemary, lavender; periwinkle, the white, the purple, and the blue; germander, flags; orange-trees, lemon-trees; and myrtles, if they be stoved; and sweet marjoram, warm set. There followeth, for the latter part of January and February, the mezereon-tree, which then blossoms; crocus vernus both the yellow and the grey; primroses, anemones, the early tulippa, hyacinthus orientalis, chamaïris, fritillaria. For March, there come violets, specially the single blue, which are the earliest; the yellow daffodil, the daisy, the almond-tree in blossom, the peach-tree in blossom, the cornelian-tree in blossom, sweet-briar. In April follow the double white violet, the wall-flower, the stock-

gillyflower, the cowslip, flower-de-luces, and lilies of all
natures; rosemary flowers, the tulippa, the double peony,
the pale daffodil, the French honeysuckle; the cherry-tree
in blossom, the damson and plum-trees in blossom, the
white-thorn in leaf, the lilac-tree. In May and June come
pinks of all sorts, specially the blush pink; roses of all
kinds, except the musk, which comes later; honeysuckles,
strawberries, bugloss, columbine; the French marigold,
flos Africanus: cherry-tree in fruit, ribes, figs in fruit,
rasps, vine-flowers, lavender in flowers; the sweet satyr-
ian, with the white flower; herba muscaria, lilium convallium, the apple-tree in blossom. In July come gillyflowers
of all varieties, musk-roses, the lime-tree in blossom,
early pears and plums in fruit, jennetings, codlins. In
August come plums of all sorts in fruit, pears, apricots,
barberries, filberts, musk-melons, monk-hoods of all
colours. In September come grapes, apples, poppies of
all colours, peaches, melocotones, nectarines, cornelians,
wardens, quinces. In October and the beginning of November come services, medlars, bullaces, roses cut or
removed to come late, hollyhocks, and such like. These
particulars are for the climate of London; but my meaning is perceived, that you may have *ver perpetuum*
[perpetual spring], as the place affords.

And because the breath of flowers is far sweeter in
the air (where it comes and goes like the warbling of
music) than in the hand, therefore nothing is more fit
for that delight than to know what be the flowers and
plants that do best perfume the air. Roses, damask and
red, are fast flowers of their smells, so that you may walk
by a whole row of them, and find nothing of their

sweetness, yea, though it be in a morning's dew. Bays likewise yield no smell as they grow, rosemary little, nor sweet marjoram. That which above all others yields the sweetest smell in the air is the violet, specially the white double violet, which comes twice a year, about the middle of April, and about Bartholomew-tide. Next to that is the musk-rose. Then the strawberry-leaves dying, with a most excellent cordial smell. Then the flower of the vines; it is a little dust, like the dust of a bent, which grows upon the cluster in the first coming forth. Then sweet-briar. Then wall-flowers, which are very delightful to be set under a parlour or lower chamber window. Then pinks and gilly-flowers, specially the matted pink and clove gillyflower. Then the flowers of the lime-tree. Then the honeysuckles, so they be somewhat afar off. Of bean-flowers I speak not, because they are field flowers. But those which perfume the air most delightfully, not passed by as the rest, but being trodden upon and crushed, are three: that is, burnet, wild thyme, and water-mints. Therefore you are to set whole alleys of them, to have the pleasure when you walk or tread.

For gardens (speaking of those which are indeed prince-like, as we have done of buildings), the contents ought not well to be under thirty acres of ground, and to be divided into three parts: a green in the entrance; a heath or desert in the going forth; and the main garden in the midst; besides alleys on both sides. And I like well that four acres of ground be assigned to the green, six to the heath, four and four to either side, and twelve to the main garden. The green hath two pleasures: the one, because nothing is more pleasant to the eye than green grass kept finely shorn; the other, because it will give you a fair alley in the midst by which you may go in front upon a stately hedge, which is to enclose the garden. But because the alley will be long, and, in great heat of the year or day, you ought not to buy the shade in the garden by going in the sun thorough the green, therefore you are, of either side the green, to plant a covert alley upon carpenter's work, about twelve foot in height, by which you may go in shade into the garden. As for the making of knots or figures with divers coloured earths, that they may lie under the windows of the house on that side which the garden stands, they be but toys: you may see as good sights many times in tarts. The garden is best to be square, encompassed on all the four sides with a stately arched hedge, the arches to be upon pillars of carpenter's work, of some ten foot high and six foot broad, and the spaces between of the same dimension with the breadth of the arch. Over the arches let there be an entire hedge of some four foot high, framed also upon carpenter's work; and upon the upper hedge, over every arch, a little turret, with a belly, enough to receive a cage of birds; and over every space between the arches some other little figure, with broad plates of round coloured glass, gilt, for the sun to play upon. But this hedge I intend to be raised upon a bank, not steep, but gently slope, of some six foot, set all with flowers. Also I understand that this square of the garden should not be the whole breadth of the ground, but to leave on either side ground enough for diversity of side alleys, unto which the two covert alleys of the green may deliver you. But there must be no alleys with hedges at either end of this great enclosure: not at the hither end, for letting your prospect upon this fair hedge from the green; nor at the further end, for letting your prospect from the hedge, through the arches, upon the heath.

For the ordering of the ground within the great hedge, I leave it to variety of device, advising nevertheless that whatsoever form you cast it into, first, it be not too busy or full of work. Wherein I, for my part, do not like images cut out in juniper or other garden stuff: they be for children. Little low hedges, round, like welts, with some pretty pyramides, I like well; and in some places, fair columns upon frames of carpenter's work. I would also have the alleys spacious and fair. You may have closer alleys upon the side grounds, but none in the main garden. I wish also, in the very middle, a fair mount, with three ascents and alleys, enough for four to walk abreast; which I would have to be perfect circles, without any bulwarks or embossments; and the whole mount to be thirty foot high; and some fine banqueting-house, with some chimneys neatly cast, and without too much glass.

For fountains, they are a great beauty and refreshment; but pools mar all, and make the garden unwholesome and full of flies and frogs. Fountains I intend to be of two natures: the one, that sprinkleth or spouteth water, the other, a fair receipt of water, of some thirty or forty foot square, but without fish or slime or mud. For the first, the ornaments of images gilt or of marble, which are in use, do well: but the main matter is so to convey the water as it never stay, either in the bowls or in the cistern; that the water be never by rest discoloured, green or red or the like, or gather any mossiness or putrefaction. Besides that, it is to be cleansed every day by the hand. Also some steps up to it, and some fine pavement about it, doth well. As for the other kind of fountain, which we may call a bathing-pool, it may admit much curiosity and beauty, wherewith we will not trouble ourselves: as that the bottom be finely paved, and with images, the sides likewise; and withal embellished with coloured glass, and such things of lustre; encompassed also with fine rails of low statuas. But the main point is the same which we mentioned in the former kind of fountain, which is that the water be in perpetual motion, fed by a water higher than the pool and delivered into it by fair spouts, and then discharged away under ground by some equality of bores, that it stay little. And for fine devices, of arching water without spilling, and making it rise in several forms (of feathers, drinking-glasses, canopies, and the like), they be pretty things to look on, but nothing to health and sweetness.

For the heath, which was the third part of our plot, I wish it to be framed, as much as may be, to a natural wildness. Trees I would have none in it, but some thickets, made only of sweet-briar and honeysuckle, and some wild vine amongst; and the ground set with violets, strawberries, and primroses. For these are sweet, and prosper in the shade. And these to be in the heath, here and there, not in any order. I like also little heaps, in the nature of mole-hills (such as are in wild heaths), to be set, some with wild thyme; some with pinks; some with germander, that gives a good flower to the eye; some with periwinkle; some with violets; some with strawberries;

some with cowslips; some with daisies; some with red roses; some with lilium convallium; some with sweet-williams red; some with bear's-foot; and the like low flowers, being withal sweet and sightly. Part of which heaps to be with standards of little bushes pricked upon their top, and part without. The standards to be roses, juniper, holly, barberries (but here and there, because of the smell of their blossom), red currants, gooseberries, rosemary, bays, sweet-briar, and such like. But these standards to be kept with cutting, that they grow not out of course.

For the side grounds, you are to fill them with variety of alleys, private, to give a full shade, some of them, wheresoever the sun be. You are to frame some of them likewise for shelter, that when the wind blows sharp you may walk as in a gallery. And those alleys must be likewise hedged at both ends, to keep out the wind; and these closer alleys must be ever finely gravelled, and no grass, because of going wet. In many of these alleys likewise, you are to set fruit-trees of all sorts, as well upon the walls as in ranges. And this would be generally observed, that the borders wherein you plant your fruit-trees be fair and large, and low, and not steep, and set with fine flowers, but thin and sparingly, lest they deceive the trees. At the end of both the side grounds, I would have a mount of some pretty height, leaving the wall of the enclosures breast high, to look abroad into the fields.

For the main garden, I do not deny but there should be some fair alleys ranged on both sides with fruit-trees, and some pretty tufts of fruit-trees, and arbours with seats, set in some decent order; but these to be by no means set too thick, but to leave the main garden so as it be not close, but the air open and free. For as for shade, I would have you rest upon the alleys of the side grounds, there to walk, if you be disposed, in the heat of the year or day; but to make account that the main garden is for the more temperate parts of the year, and, in the heat of summer, for the morning and the evening, or overcast days.

For aviaries, I like them not, except they be of that largeness as they may be turfed, and have living plants and bushes set in them; that the birds may have more scope and natural nestling, and that no foulness appear in the floor of the aviary. So I have made a platform of a princely garden, partly by precept, partly by drawing, not a model, but some general lines of it; and in this I have spared for no cost. But it is nothing for great princes, that for the most part taking advice with workmen, with no less cost set their things together; and sometimes add statuas and such things for state and magnificence, but nothing to the true pleasure of a garden.

Of Negotiating

It is generally better to deal by speech than by letter, and by the mediation of a third than by a man's self. Letters are good when a man would draw an answer by letter back again, or when it may serve for a man's justification afterwards to produce his own letter, or where it may be danger to be interrupted or heard by pieces. To deal in person is good when a man's face breedeth regard, as commonly with inferiors, or in tender cases, where a man's eye upon the countenance of him with whom he speaketh may give him a direction how far to go; and generally, where a man will reserve to himself liberty either to disavow or to expound. In choice of instruments, it is better to choose men of a plainer sort, that are like to do that that is committed to them, and to report back again faithfully the success, than those that are cunning to contrive out of other men's business somewhat to grace themselves, and will help the matter in report for satisfaction sake. Use also such persons as affect the business wherein they are employed, for that quickeneth much; and such as are fit for the matter, as bold men for expostulation, fair-spoken men for persuasion, crafty men for inquiry and observation, froward and absurd men for business that doth not well bear out itself. Use also such as have been lucky and prevailed before in things wherein you have employed them; for that breeds confidence, and they will strive to maintain their prescription. It is better to sound a person with whom one deals afar off, than to fall upon the point at first, except you mean to surprise him by some short question. It is better dealing with men in appetite, than with those that are where they would be. If a man deal with another upon conditions, the start or first performance is all; which a man cannot reasonably demand, except either the nature of the thing be such which must go before; or else a man can persuade the other party that he shall still need him in some other thing; or else that he be counted the honester man. All practice is to discover, or to work. Men discover themselves in trust, in passion, at unawares, and of necessity, when they would have somewhat done and cannot find an apt pretext. If you would work any man, you must either know his nature and fashions and so lead him; or his ends, and so persuade him; or his weakness and disadvantages, and so awe him; or those that have interest in him, and so govern him. In dealing with cunning persons, we must ever consider their ends, to interpret their speeches; and it is good to say little to them, and that which they least look for. In all negotiations of difficulty, a man may not look to sow and reap at once, but must prepare business, and so ripen it by degrees.

Of Suitors

Many ill matters and projects are undertaken, and private suits do putrefy the public good. Many good matters are undertaken with bad minds; I mean not only corrupt minds, but crafty minds that intend not performance. Some embrace suits which never mean to deal effectually in them, but if they see there may be life in the matter by some other mean, they will be content to win a thank, or take a second reward, or at least to make use in the meantime of the suitor's hopes. Some take hold of suits only for an occasion to cross some other; or to make an information whereof they could not otherwise have apt pretext, without care what become of the suit when that turn is served; or generally to make other men's business a kind of entertainment to bring in their own. Nay, some undertake suits with a full purpose to let them fall, to the end to gratify the adverse party or competitor. Surely there is in some sort a right in every suit; either a right of equity, if it be a suit of controversy, or a right of desert, if it be a suit of petition. If affection lead a man to favour the wrong side in justice, let him rather use his countenance to compound the matter than to carry it. If affection lead a man to favour the less worthy in desert, let him do it without depraving or disabling the better deserver. In suits which a man doth not well understand, it is good to refer them to some friend of trust and judgement, that may report whether he may deal in them with honour; but let him choose well his referendaries, for else he may be led by the nose. Suitors are so distasted with delays and abuses, that plain dealing, in denying to deal in suits at first, and reporting the success barely, and in challenging no more thanks than one hath deserved, is grown not only honourable, but also gracious. In suits of favour, the first coming ought to take little place. So far forth consideration may be had of his trust, that if intelligence of the matter could not otherwise have been had but by him, advantage be not taken of the note but the party left to his other means, and in some sort recompensed for his discovery. To be ignorant of the value of a suit is simplicity; as well as to be ignorant of the right thereof is want of conscience. Secrecy in suits is a great mean of obtaining, for voicing them to be in forwardness may discourage some kind of suitors, but doth quicken and awake others. But timing of the suit is the principal. Timing, I say, not only in respect of the person that should grant it, but in respect of those which are like to cross it. Let a man, in the choice of his mean, rather choose the fittest mean than the greatest mean, and rather them that deal in certain things than those that are general. The reparation of a denial is sometimes equal to the first grant, if a man show himself neither dejected nor discontented. *Iniquum petas, ut aequum feras* [Ask for more than what is just, so that you may get your due]* is a good rule where a man hath strength of favour, but otherwise a man were better

* Quintilian, *The Education of an Orator*, IV.5.16.

rise in his suit, for he that would have ventured at first to have lost the suitor, will not in the conclusion lose both the suitor and his own former favour. Nothing is thought so easy a request to a great person as his letter, and yet if it be not in a good cause it is so much out of his reputation. There are no worse instruments than these general contrivers of suits; for they are but a kind of poison and infection to public proceedings.

Of Studies

Studies serve for delight, for ornament, and for ability. Their chief use for delight, is in privateness and retiring; for ornament, is in discourse; and for ability, is in the judgement and disposition of business. For expert men can execute, and perhaps judge of particulars, one by one; but the general counsels, and the plots and marshalling of affairs come best from those that are learned. To spend too much time in studies is sloth; to use them too much for ornament is affectation; to make judgement wholly by their rules is the humour of a scholar. They perfect nature, and are perfected by experience, for natural abilities are like natural plants that need proyning by study; and studies themselves do give forth directions too much at large, except they be bounded in by experience. Crafty men contemn studies, simple men admire them, and wise men use them; for they teach not their own use; but that is a wisdom without them and above them, won by observation. Read not to contradict and confute; nor to believe and take for granted; nor to find talk and discourse; but to weigh and consider. Some books are to be tasted, others to be swallowed, and some few to be chewed and digested: that is, some books are to be read only in parts; others to be read, but not curiously; and some few to be read wholly and with diligence and attention. Some books also may be read by deputy, and extracts made of them by others, but that would be only in the less important arguments, and the meaner sort of books; else distilled books are like common distilled waters, flashy things. Reading maketh a full man; conference a ready man; and writing an exact man. And therefore, if a man write little, he had need have a great memory; if he confer little, he had need have a present wit; and if he read little, he had need have much cunning, to seem to know that he doth not. Histories make men wise, poets witty, the mathematics subtle, natural philosophy deep, moral grave, logic and rhetoric able to contend. *Abeunt studia in mores* [Studies go to make up a man's character].* Nay, there is no stond or impediment in the wit but may be wrought out by fit studies, like as diseases of the body may have appropriate exercises. Bowling is good for the stone and reins; shooting for the lungs and breast; gentle walking for the stomach; riding for the head; and the like. So if a man's wit be wandering, let him study the mathematics; for in demonstrations, if his wit be called away never so little, he must begin again. If his wit be not apt to distinguish or find differences, let him study the Schoolmen, for they are *cymini sectores* [hairsplitters]. If he be not apt to beat over matters, and to call up one thing to prove and illustrate another, let him study the lawyers' cases. So every defect of the mind may have a special receipt.

* Ovid, *Heroides*, XV.83.

Of Vainglory

It was prettily devised of Aesop,* *The fly sat upon the axle-tree of the chariot wheel, and said, 'What a dust do I raise!'* So are there some vain persons that, whatsoever goeth alone or moveth upon greater means, if they have never so little hand in it, they think it is they that carry it. They that are glorious must needs be factious, for all bravery stands upon comparisons. They must needs be violent to make good their own vaunts. Neither can they be secret, and therefore not effectual, but according to the French proverb, *Beaucoup de bruit, peu de fruit: much bruit, little fruit.* Yet certainly there is use of this quality in civil affairs. Where there is an opinion and fame to be created, either of virtue or greatness, these men are good trumpeters. Again, as Titus Livius noteth in the case of Antiochus and the Aetolians,† *There are sometimes great effects of cross lies*, as, if a man that negotiates between two princes to draw them to join in a war against the third, doth extol the forces of either of them above measure, the one to the other: and sometimes he that deals between man and man raiseth his own credit with both by pretending greater interest than he hath in either.

* Not Aesop, but Lorenzo Bevilaqua.
† Antiochus, King of Syria, allied with the Aetolians against Rome, but was defeated. See Livy, *History*, XXXV.12 and 17–18.

And in these and the like kinds, it often falls out that somewhat is produced of nothing, for lies are sufficient to breed opinion, and opinion brings on substance. In militar commanders and soldiers, vainglory is an essential point, for as iron sharpens iron, so by glory one courage sharpeneth another. In cases of great enterprise, upon charge and adventure, a composition of glorious natures doth put life into business, and those that are of solid and sober natures have more of the ballast than of the sail. In fame of learning, the flight will be slow without some feathers of ostentation. *Qui de contemnenda gloria libros scribunt, nomen suum inscribunt* [Men who write books on the worthlessness of glory take care to put their names on the title-page].* Socrates, Aristotle, Galen, were men full of ostentation. Certainly vainglory helpeth to perpetuate a man's memory, and virtue was never so beholding to human nature, as it received his due at the second hand. Neither had the fame of Cicero, Seneca, Plinius Secundus, borne her age so well, if it had not been joined with some vanity in themselves: like unto varnish, that makes ceilings not only shine but last. But all this while, when I speak of vainglory, I mean not of that property that Tacitus doth attribute to Mucianus, *Omnium quae dixerat feceratque arte quadam ostentator* [He had a certain skill of displaying to advantage all that he had said or done],† for that proceeds not of vanity, but of natural magnanimity and discretion, and in some persons is not only comely, but gracious. For excusations,

* From Cicero, *Tusculan Disputations*, I.15.
† From *Histories*, II.80.

cessions, modesty itself well governed, are but arts of ostentation. And amongst those arts there is none better than that which Plinius Secundus speaketh of, which is to be liberal of praise and commendation to others, in that wherein a man's self hath any perfection. For saith Pliny very wittily: *In commending another you do yourself right, for he that you commend is either superior to you in that you commend, or inferior. If he be inferior, if he be to be commended, you much more; if he be superior, if he be not to be commended, you much less.** Glorious men are the scorn of wise men, the admiration of fools, the idols of parasites, and the slaves of their own vaunts.

---

* From *Letters*, VI.17.4.

Of Anger

To seek to extinguish anger utterly is but a bravery of the Stoics. We have better oracles: *Be angry, but sin not. Let not the sun go down upon your anger.* Anger must be limited and confined, both in race and in time. We will first speak how the natural inclination and habit to be angry may be attempered and calmed. Secondly, how the particular motions of anger may be repressed, or at least refrained from doing mischief. Thirdly, how to raise anger or appease anger in another.

For the first: there is no other way but to meditate and ruminate well upon the effects of anger, how it troubles man's life. And the best time to do this is to look back upon anger when the fit is throughly over. Seneca saith well that *anger is like ruin, which breaks itself upon that it falls.*[*] The Scripture exhorteth us *to possess our souls in patience.*[†] Whosoever is out of patience is out of possession of his soul. Men must not turn bees,

> *animasque in vulnere ponunt.*
> [and lay down their lives in the wound.][‡]

Anger is certainly a kind of baseness; as it appears well

---

[*] *On Anger*, I.1.2.   [†] See Luke 21.19.
[‡] Virgil, *Georgics*, IV.238.

in the weakness of those subjects in whom it reigns: children, women, old folks, sick folks. Only men must beware that they carry their anger rather with scorn than with fear, so that they may seem rather to be above the injury than below it: which is a thing easily done if a man will give law to himself in it.

For the second point: the causes and motives of anger are chiefly three. First, to be too sensible of hurt, for no man is angry that feels not himself hurt; and therefore tender and delicate persons must needs be oft angry, they have so many things to trouble them which more robust natures have little sense of. The next is the apprehension and construction of the injury offered to be, in the circumstances thereof, full of contempt; for contempt is that which putteth an edge upon anger, as much or more than the hurt itself. And therefore, when men are ingenious in picking out circumstances of contempt, they do kindle their anger much. Lastly, opinion of the touch of a man's reputation doth multiply and sharpen anger. Wherein the remedy is, that a man should have, as Consalvo* was wont to say, *telam honoris crassiorem* [a thicker web of honour]. But in all refrainings of anger, it is the best remedy to win time, and to make a man's self believe that the opportunity of his revenge is not yet come, but that he foresees a time for it; and so to still himself in the meantime and reserve it.

To contain anger from mischief, though it take hold of a man, there be two things whereof you must have special caution. The one, of extreme bitterness of words,

* Gonzalo, Hernandez de Cordova, Spanish general, d. 1515.

especially if they be aculeate and proper; for *communia maledicta* [general revilings] are nothing so much; and again, that in anger a man reveal no secrets, for that makes him not fit for society. The other, that you do not peremptorily break off in any business in a fit of anger; but howsoever you show bitterness, do not act anything that is not revocable.

For raising and appeasing anger in another: it is done chiefly by choosing of times, when men are frowardest and worst disposed, to incense them. Again, by gathering (as was touched before) all that you can find out to aggravate the contempt. And the two remedies are by the contraries. The former, to take good times, when first to relate to a man an angry business, for the first impression is much. And the other is to sever, as much as may be, the construction of the injury from the point of contempt, imputing it to misunderstanding, fear, passion, or what you will.